Dreamland Theatre

Caitlin Press Inc.
8100 Alderwood Road,
Halfmoon Bay, BC V0N 1Y1
www.caitlin-press.com

Text design and cover by Vici Johnstone.
Cover image courtesy The Exploration Place, Prince George, image # 2009.45.1
Printed in Canada

Caitlin Press Inc. acknowledges financial support from the Government of Canada through the Canada Book Fund and the Canada Council for the Arts, and from the Province of British Columbia through the British Columbia Arts Council and the Book Publisher's Tax Credit.

Library and Archives Canada Cataloguing in Publication

Budde, Robert, 1966-, author

Dreamland Theatre / Rob Budde.

Poems.

ISBN 978-1-927575-45-1 (bound)

I. Title.

PS8553.U446D74 2014   C811'.54   C2013-908555-6

poems

Rob Budde

DREAMLAND THEATRE

CAITLIN PRESS

for Hoolghulh

Table of Contents

dreamland mapping

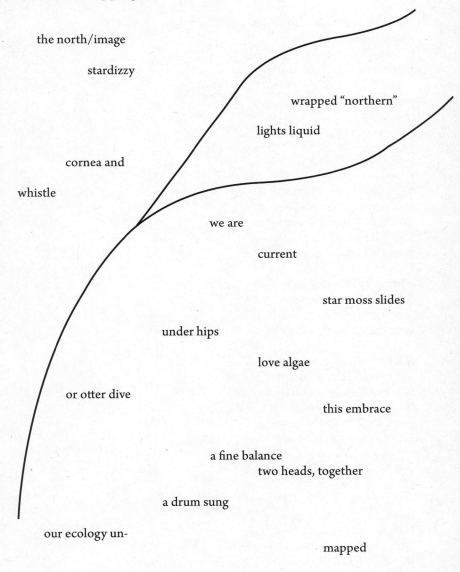

the north/image

stardizzy

wrapped "northern"

lights liquid

cornea and

whistle

we are

current

star moss slides

under hips

love algae

or otter dive

this embrace

a fine balance

two heads, together

a drum sung

our ecology un-

mapped

follow the crabapple blossom smell

not saying the word reliably, historically
like weather or the knots
in thinking around
emotional language, tangled
in this bright mid-day moment (of reading)
and the medium
and a pronoun ...

and "you" is never easy —
a striated sign of things
to come and counter
to the sense of sentences, its ease
and assurance — so the word
"with" becomes still uneasier and
I walk into the sunlit room,
poem in hand, a proximity,
molecular and climatic,
twined and tugging tight
half listening to the news
of storms forming
over the warming oceans ...

a deligitimized ground, standing
there, as if through some accuracy
of scientific instrumentation, who
is who's target is the question and
the water line wavers in the re
calculations — you look up your altitude
in an archaic book of symbols,
you look up and tell me we need
to flee ...

love is resistant to anti-
biotics, bodies react to themselves
and become something else; later
we hear 21st century love retreated from the coasts,

subsided in the mountains, subsisted
on salmon and blueberries ...

we read "faith" in the remaining
records — but these codes
fail, these letters fall still, cars by the side
of the highway house
sparrows and squirrels,
a reorganized polis ...

and I'd like to think
of us, by the side of the derelict
highway, bereft and happy,
a fistful of yarrow and a wooden cup of tea

the future tense may
be the poem's love sprung
from the old language

1912 theatre

a text of pleasure or a text
of bliss with mixed maps —
races and names —
what tradition holds you
guides the form
forms the guide

(the imagined black and white photo)
the white-sided building on skids in the rain, in
the mud, pulled by a team of horses

moving Dreamland Theatre, moving
day, 1912, from one side
of the townsite to the other

stage cracking

and to what end does that image
lead? what narrative sunk
in mud and propped
by wooden planks

the tableau is narrow, determined,
and the rest is not worthy of a picture,
or outside the picture, or watching
from the woods as the trees fall

the grand cover of culture;
an architectural path pulls
bodies, now groaning uphill

now wondering where am I
looking from and on what
land am I standing?

'en cha khuna'

       Nechako and Fraser, two
languages and a third
discovery, on the south-
side portage: a recollection, a passage
moving on

       or staying
by need or want, the provisions
carried from the west
the salmon run, grease, at least then
east through the passes to Beaver

       on that day
in 1907, I would say to you
'snachailya, musicho'
as a guest and co-explorer
of inside

       gold and horses
cross paths with the soft-speakers
the ash of ancestors misread
and the language crashes in
from Boston

       the plateau
of watersheds, neural directions
we take from topography,
wood a texture against our backs
as we rest, historicize, work

       in a different economy,
a training of tongues to
carry this wet 'lh', or
a collective barrier protecting
this lake, these rivers, this place:
a body placed in harm's way

up here where
there is no pressure to conform
to urban forms — here, identity is
a new stride, cleaner, smarter
and knowing how to say it

through the valley of the high light

on the road to the downsized pulp mill
past the oxeye daisies, five or ten
in a clump in the gravel dust
piling on the leaves and petals

alder and cottonwood saplings
shining in the too-hot sun clinging
to the cutbanks and riverbanks
and the road's cracked asphalt
gleams with the residue of tar and metal

the sound of the Nechako is lost in the blare
of trucks and the glare of the windshields
pass along the far shore where a few
young pines survive and lean over the railway tracks

a bald eagle might pass over but not today —
if there are salmon they would have snuck by
months ago — so crows play in the hot
updrafts and a boy pedals down to look for
saskatoons and room to think of something new

poetry travels, a freak hobo

traffic traffic and food money and language and bowels.

it is all about waste, the vagrant says, gesturing
toward somewhere else.

poetry is a dangerous
retention like cities without air and something
needs to give.

the word 'plum' is about
where it's from. the wanderer asks
a grocer, receives little or no information,
opens the next book.

a cleansing, the hobo hears his friend say.
a cleansing, the hobo thinks and forgets
his wallet, the store's location, the shape
of arugula, why he can't be far from
the truth or its proxy ...

a cleansing, and he remembers what he needed
and writes about syntax and
walks to give it to his friend.

home, cottage, woods

there is this
place, inside
plied with hemlock
logs fitted care-
fully in a hut-
shaped life
with you

the pond and babbling
stream nearby would tremble
with births and deaths
and the garden begins again
every spring sprawling
mint and bright
broccoli heads and chuckles
of brussel sprouts

the small clearing against the forest
boughs against the misinformed highway

learning would be sunset and rest the rainy day
the hillside store of huckleberries, an evening show
the lake osprey dive

the hut, a heart
its hearth waiting
warm where inhibitions
have lately left
and leaves line our lives

there is this place:
a hut-shaped idea
just around that bend
in thinking

how I joined the seal herd too

> *I learned*
> *it was not I*

to let my body give
who controlled the rocks

— Robert Kroetsch (1927-2011)

for an instant   I thought
of the difference between   air and
without thinking   her flipper
buoyed me   out of
gender and the institution   was
what   I forgot

ankle turned   into the fin
I always wanted   to know
something other   than air
float   belly-centered in love

and it was not difficult   this
landlessness   at the pivot
of our dance   what matters
what touches   in what language

when the others join   too
the curbs and spiral stairways
will all dissolve into   swirls
of joy and   breaches

and when I spun   surfing
in the blue-grey   to look
surprised   at her eyes   she
even more   surprised was
there too   really   really

the waters were   words mostly
verbs of being   ecstatic   and
I did not miss   my groin
at all   sleek we swam   away

iceflows and schools of   ideas
art and movement   through liquid
ease she teases and   swims better
than I ever   dreamed

another state of   being
intimate with   oneself   water
a wet embrace of care   full
of promise   loveswirl

and swerve   you   sped
ahead and   I   learning
floundered after   eyes
finding new   colours the shape
of longing   receding

a moment of doubt   would
you leave   adrift   I wonder
how would I find land again   but
my body knows now   it will not
turns back   arched   in deep
dives   deeper

where currents meet   and fishes
are rich   we reached   fins skyward
stretching the surface of the
possible   beach pebbles against
skin a sound of   release

leaving the wabbling wake of
past lives   land-bound slow
walkers and linear   thinking
maybe you and I   maybe

water riffled around   our discourse
of love bubbling with the   future
my sore ears disappeared   overused
to the inane blathering of news

paper fell apart   paint ran
books disintegrated into soggy messes of intention
clothes dissolved into   sensation
our house became the many
horizons   prismed by light
became a progress toward

the slurry

as ideas move across, a wet inter-
action will form, made
of material from the sharpening
mind and the listener — it is junk
remains in the poem to facilitate
slippage and friction

as the moisture in the language
drops, it is crucial that it be kept wet,
slurry re-applied to the reading act because
it contains all the particles — the pieces and fragments
shift shift shift of thought up until that point in the
text — and so will sound
out meaning: fine, keen, ready to work
out there

speaking in english

I have these
voices in my blood that sang me sitting here
                                                    — John Lent

you could walk along an avenue here,
many places actually, and there would appear,
unmagically asphalt and road signs and
houses, large and small, and a store
and another (a pedestrian — "hello") and
another (this one selling something you need
to go with the stuff the first one is selling)
and a restaurant and another,
a government office, a police station…
well, you get the picture

you could walk along an avenue here,
unmagically, and begin to peel away
its imposition, to trace the paths
of its assertion, to unearth (much like
an unearthed mass grave that had gone
unrecorded) the measures of violence
that made this avenue you walk

you could walk differently along this
incline of forgotten waterways
and smell the uprooted vegetation
notice a furtive movement here
a motion that is magically you.

turn left on george st.

the standing address, naked and constitutional
mirrored or thinking of one — one —
self many times: the thick air, re mind
divided between affiliations/mind
an ecology

independence a vitamin
or waterway erosion
the force of dissatisfaction turned

lovewords and *systembreaking*
and breath

such an address's
mediation is the subject — classrooms waver —
20th century bodies are new and
old — the text of skin, skin of
text's bones, bones of one's own senses coursed ("all" and
"you" – Fr.) into 1st street discourses
with rules, miscreants, war ...

if there is a narrative it is recurring and
repressive; if there is a poetic it is
non-industrial food and an indefinite
expenditure

meaning/gender: in it
doing nothing worthwhile

for me, the body is a metaphor of energy, intensity

khasdzoon yusk'ut

walking with Ken
down Victoria, or up the hill
through crescents to Central, the powers
tilted away from speech
before it is and then
rethinking why

Cranbrook Hill by the Dakelh name
and the cutbanks surround
the cupped hands
taking and giving
while Ken speaks of outside, the Nass
and Blackwater where the mountains
are reflected, uncertainty and systems
begin to inform the masses

I would not want to be
anywhere else but walking
with Ken, thinking about how
to stand and not betray

— if we were on a lake
it would be in a strong, well-made
canoe unlike the one
I leave in the yard unwritten

ashes across the pass

the sound of land, wet and
stopped, alternating
language and substance, subject
and object, lost
in a host's presence

and how he greets you —
the welcome is
stone glottal and aspirant
wistful over the river

(but that river bend, that one
over past the joining, that one is
not for you)

problem: standing on the ground   (yun)
double dawning like that other
idea spoken to you and   ('ust'oh)   you are

like days of the week and work
ethic and the lord's order/layers
of speech when the young girl says
she is not coming home

the language comes like (I am)
a four-year-old

an uncertain anger for a verb
its sound eluding your tongue

$1.99 garage sale map

How must it be
to be caught in the Empire, to have
everything you do matter?
                    — John Newlove

the forecast is for
castes of greater and lesser
and the charts glaze over
with want

the bubble is water and air;
the tipping point is a mean temperature

hedges are like properly broken
lines — in keeping with property values
but the risk is not yours

bookings are accessed by writers
of wealth and exemptions abound
in derivative contracts, leverage, recognizable
structures and the liquidity of investment
in the empire

no need to listen: certainty surrounds the old
economy — playing with oneself
has always been a good bet

self-absorption is a hemispheric
phenomenon and cancels out
the emotional use of language
and how it addresses the animal

futures, forwards, options and swaps
are the only way one line can move to the next
in the empire —
pyramids cover with sand

unless the word has no operating
leverage, I have no interest in its
profit, poetic value has no
place in reasons for imaginary debt

and so, eventually, comes clean

rumble strip

1.

(#16 along the north flowing Fraser)

down there, the surface turbulence
of water a chute
of large boulders
flow flow flow the river
cajoles roll roll roll
and all around ocean
ocean ocean chants the road —

2.

(#5 along the North Thompson)

'some johnny appleseed' planting
aesthetics around ranch-houses,
corrals, the lippy yellow
of the weeping ornamental —
that one there —

3.

(#97 south of Kamloops)

goddamn big car — why don't we
wade through conservatism
at that shallow spot
look from the other shore
another like that other
one —

4.

(#97 south of Vernon)

passing the slow
into slower like caricatures
that agribusiness has drained
into the lake

I can't believe this ravenous
road anymore — it is not
viable, its shoulder emblems
and codes — so I am suspended
a low vibration, set to
roll roll roll

decommissioning naver creek road

that part human made
dammed or cut, a lack
of flow in the elements of knowledge
relegated to charts and boardroom
sludge, tailings and run-off clogged
with the residue of ire

to remove the road's meaning

700 road to the Ahbau turnoff
and willow river cutblocks
from here to there the trans-
port a running over, a spill-
way tread deep into the layered
stories of who and what before

rail, pipe, asphalt, ATV
tracks all to get what's to be got
out of other concerns duly
noted in the consultation process

that living flow is nonhuman
made and divisible by measures,
an unknown technology and
narrative turn just where the road
thought it was stable, before the new
(washout)
mythology told it why.

trapline routes

at the top is the bad
boy; shit and wasted energy, broken faucets barely
filter down to the small towns, marshy
stacks of manuscripts, the empty library reading
room, coffee bogs, and parties no one
is invited to

a blue-green algae territorial bloom:
a flush of meaning-excess, an unbalanced
distribution of print, a sucking out of nutrients

the imprint is mean, a scar
of text to assert territory where it
means business, class, a parachute clause
to let the CEO go

the blossom is a base
insecurity, a buyout for the prose
class — a sign, a structure
that wasn't one before
the green slick

poison spit into the magazines,
the blogs, the policies of heritage and
origins — it cannot be stemmed,
this riot of male monotheism —

the others, the women and brown faces,
shift to the treeline where
no one goes, where writing is antlered,
untouristed, uninteresting

graduate school greenway

ungulate blood
made the map inconclusive and where
we were was a matter of
conversation, gesture, weather

the mother was looking not
for us but for shelter from
our knowing
anything

the books were still

the dull red spots in the snow
are not a cipher but the first
thing that a new world would know

circle dance (pine center mall 2020)

nearing this heft, nearing
tides and lamplight and
accumulated heirlooms placed
in a row, tambourine-like, against
the pressure of outside, out
of hearing, struck instead
by the riotous friction of cells
on cells, hunger, tissue rustling
just to the left of profound — and
silence is cradled in your impossible mouth
a wordless o obediently biting
off a reply to propriety, a vital levity
in the parabolic viscera, those homey
keys to absolute knowing, knowing
your voice should be going back to the beginning,
should be nosing a nostalgic scent in the fabric,
should be resolutely circling away
from the already known.

double me down 10th ave.

quick one two push
off and hey move
eyes back on the road and
stop giggling
okay not
too fast

the words turning
as we go
downtown when it's
sunny and down-
hill and not too
car-filled

is it you steering or
me wishing
you would

turn and kiss
my cheek
because of something
we've discovered
about ethics

caring about language
emissions and how

we, careening
got there

downtown revitalization

therapy for the rescued
handouts and a reconnection
to the river, assessments
of who is here and why

the heights harbour such
tax relief

the car no longer keyed
conversations begin on George St.
where none were before

it begins partly in a townhouse
on Spruce where awareness
is assembled on corkboard

it begins with that early contradiction:
love for the violent place,
the men who left, the women
who took over

like millworkers and treeplanters
eyeing one another at
Second Cup — a culpability
and an invitation over —
the first question being
'what's going on out there?'

skytongue and speaking west

it takes the whole afternoon in
Prince George, gorging myself on
Victoria, Queensway, Ospika buildings,
flecks of moisture and rain a rinse a slow
groaning into hills, arch, the rise of river

rub along esker, Connaught
caught between teeth and tongue, thighs
roll over nechako

it's an utterance, a long vowel sound,
a low growling howl, a shout to the 15th ave. traffic letting
go of clothes and conscience the valley
a cup and taste
taste tip and pluck a wedge
seeping into salt and books
my mouth puffing wide inside
this evergreen bush this word
tangle this cutbank curl

it takes all afternoon, takes
soft soft taste softly laid
this poem tensing on Prince George

a kitchen on tabor blvd

1.

as if composed for finality —
this text intransitive, just that, but a translation across
an unending ease, the way we
speak without thinking, sentences
of clutter unedited, why
we pretend to have only one mouth

2.

and burning the pastry, bumping into things is
exactly about poetry, attention, frantic
chance or passion, this is
what might be left behind, a phonetic souvenir
because too much was assumed
about sound across space —
what interrupts is sacred

3.

campy, corduroy, and rounding
off at the nearest line break, only
waiting for the other to intervene
like an unrequited shove, veering off
beat and your mind is of two
and then more

4.

affinity to clusters, stop, stop,
the clatter of shoes, polyester, long
vowels for tonal coherence, the gender off octave
unavailable, draft dodging the lyric sense
to stay put, introspection, spinning wheels while
(smoke alarm) these circumspect intentions suit this fling fine

5.

interval and clause, the last
weave or glance not *film noire*, that face in a
black and white word, the voice grainy
a possibility of rain, technology,
the crowd on the tv breathes, moisture, sigh, sign, our lungs
dual radials for traction, nowhere to go but in

a collect call from here

staying close to home, home
troubling the most basic signals

trying not to write the next
either a blade, or branch, or imprint in snow

careful journal taking
observances made but not made out

uniforms would not be involved
the first sentence of the story is enough

posing, a kind of posture, unassuming
being asked into the gang and declining

to trouble the next line
careful observances of blade or branch

staying close, calling this way
giving it space to splay

water across a smooth trunk or sound
either journal or poetry will do

repetitions imprinted on each meeting
trying not to decline the next place, close

the first reform vote was lost, intentionally
being asked home and knowing it

the story assumes a posture, knowing
made but not fully known, calling

panago pizza, westwood drive

older now, cognizant of commerce
base and superstructure service
the pizza guy of back then
rebellious against the sure thing
in everything and why not buy
a big goddamn
university degree, the canon
and all those myths out of fashion

now, the delivery guy's kids eat plain
cheese with multigrain crust

a different kind of economy, love

the pizza guy remembers the bird lady at the door
placing old coins in his palm
one at a time, slowly
reciting the full price intensely
focused hunger

"measures of wealth, well-being … "
begins to say something standing at
the corner of ethics and art
but the playoffs are on, jobs
are being cut, there is no time to think
we might be not possible

maps don't keep

gas station meat
flattened out, a red spot
splash on the highway

shapes in the cheesy logo
you trying not to stare
at the cashier's protein

using too much
b/c you don't have the right
tires and self-
gratification is easy where
living isn't

some CEO in California
is laughing at us

foods that rot quickly
are better for you;
other creatures don't want
most of the stock,
clamped shut, a sphincter
of few nutrients preserved
for archaeologists wondering
what went wrong

in the gas station, the meat seethes and
all the faces stare back at you;
the cooler fills with steamy breath
hnghgnhgnhgnhgnnggnngngngn

sweetsawtooth at the corner store

taste changes in a glut
and american buds de-
sensitize, the dumbing down
of the electorate

the food flavours haunt
a criminal malcontent
in the molars and a few
grandmothers still have their
herb gardens hidden

malnutrition is a future
of distraction, agency-
less eating into the brain
and it's raining dollars

so that dollop of grease,
that lump of white,
these polls that flatline, fall
past the last post

you'd think it would end
there, famine taking everyone.— but no,
the mouth opens the new millennium
with all that corn fructose spat out,
and then shuts up for a century

15th & mysogyny

the line gropes from
fierce engines of what they called
'desire' — pedal pressed
down driven by fossil
fuels, the gut and the same scene
thrill in the chase, a brotherhood

gang rape all Hollywood glam and king
shit strut — it's the prenorth contingencies that hold
sway, a blackwater cabal of fathers haunting
the former form and sad handmaidens
don't care that the classroom holds
them in an unwelcome gaze

the measure of risk
is his own anxieties
because the college insider
is a psychology of fear
of being
found out

cowboy hats over turned chairs, sergeant's 2005

now that you fly
fucking unhorsed and dreading the city
its airs, the propriety of lit streets
now that you drink more
to bygone glories not
your own but the idea
of frontier, the power of reins
let loose and as far as the eye can see
now that you aren't fence mending
everything is getting out
and the search gets dirty
looking angry for something as good
as poetry she-
it what does that get me?
so now that you are
up against it, how do you save
face, back down with grace or
fly at him with everything you've got
left

male subdivisions

and they take on the character of
conflict, sliding into the role as if
to say, 'here I am
apart' or something larger

the grandfather would say it
in silence and a swift
whack of power comes
with no context

the men stood around
bereft and swinging for
the fences — fame I suppose,
some sort of immortality

caught up in the sting of
knowing the pain could be lost could
be healed   under

here the men said the getting
was good and everything was
freedom which means pain
inflicted quietly, in domesticated ways

means seven of the eight readers
were men and the one woman was
coined in brass and strung out

here the men are libertine, which means
ancient and schooled in the ways of
creeping posts and grooming the style,
the candor of oppression

here the men said nothing has happened
and never will

turning off central

i am learning to cut onions with my eyes
shut. it's really quite easy, that
slow groping process, a deceleration
the sharp edge against thumb pad, the quick plunge into
flesh, the memory of tears, feeling
the wet surface sliding out layers, your fingers
slick with juice, your eyes tight, clenched,
refusing to see the effect, blur

it's really quite easy, like averting
eyes from a roadside
casualty: a squirrel, a deer,
a dog, a crumpled orange cat
a hand holding a sign reading
"help please" and it is
past, the highway straight and smooth,
just like that, quite easy

you see i am learning to cut
corners with emotions, the way they
get in the gears, slow production
sick pay, counseling, worker's comp
other such archaic salves

such a simple motion not to see
the small muscles of the eye trained
to defend, defer, hold back the swells
of dust, pain, incrimination, complicity
a crust at the corner, caught in lashes
brushed away later

i am learning to cut
down on negativity, the ugly
pictures on tv: bombings, machete
killings of all sorts, the gratuitous
mangled body of a child ripped up
by well-intentioned daisy-cutters —

these are the type of things i am learning
to ignore, shut off, it's really quite easy

you see, i am learning to cut onions with my eyes
fully shut, as if sealed with coins
it's really quite easy

mentoring the northern boy

a casual fear, familiar
almost invisibly learning to defend oneself
in grade three, fists raised like you knew
they were supposed to,
tears welling, capped

carbon copy characters —
sticks and stones will

or riding pride, a tank
decanting terror churning;
such bravery is sheer orderly panic,
a powerful but empty shell,
the fuel drying up on some conquered shore
the beast beached

or riding the oil rig
high and filled with
cash running the truck
idle and grabbing at anything
anything, a glut of purposelessness

a bull in a china shop
afraid of being laughed at

masculinity flees in face of hunger, the courageous
real, and huddles, ensconced in myth   ·

figuratively, i have no balls

ecriture feminine — another state of mind
to take us into writing
the next century

and yet i am the same scared little boy
as stephen harper —

the question becomes
how does one respond to the unknown?

place, strapped to the chest

langue wanting blood, wild-eyed,
beseeching, the form of
pronouncements, rants,
condemnations, manifestoes, those
bullets slapping against history

thirsty words like *Allah* and *Christ* —
they want something
unleashed in me and
here I slouch
reading these letters in some bar or café and I am tempted to give in
in a small way

and this is not some other place, this is Canada 2014, I am reading in English,
we are a democracy of sort, the GNP is doing fine, etc

but the body decomposes equally

left with this treachery, this rough
love, this pipe-bomb narrative, this syntax of betrayal
and a question

will you give it up?

open up to the words spoken in the hiss of truth and
spittle, release into the poetics of shame, disgust,
let disavowal guide you to a higher purpose

the poem an artistic sign of resistance
your body taken with it;
you become meaning

your body a blockade,
historic, standing in front
of a bulldozer, a pipeline
survey all but settled

because words are nails shot through
with semiotic flow

        but the pretense is too much;
        the trope is pure fantasy

but the desire, oh that moment of danger
stays — a longing in language for
elsewhere and transformation into something
horrifically memorable, a sign of change,
a semantic shift
on the late news

rivers from alberta dammed

in grade nine my grandfather gives me the .22,
tells me to practice my aim —
the gun, its giving, a sentence
with perfect grammar:
the range — syntax, my life as man,
the target — dependent object, success as a man,
the bullets — the verb, the act, actions, the motion of raising
my voice just so, an entrance/exit pattern
(the damage done — mere semantics)
the gun — the noun, the enunciation, that shadow slung over, well hung,
an inheritance (tempting heresy)
the miss — the ungrammaticality, failure, fallow, the *unmettled*
forge, the blank, a single feeble flag
sprung from the barrel, a bleating guffaw
a sob, stop, the sentence un —
i broke the gun, literally, a small part near the loading mechanism (i
refuse to look up the proper terminology) snapped when i threw it down,
shocked when i swear i saw blood on the barrel

that and a belt-buckle with a horse rearing, this
taken cumulatively, equals lineage

that passing down, passing on, passing
through my veins the impulse
like an addiction at birth

i did practice with my .22, set up clay targets and took careful aim
the gun hard against my shoulder like a hand and i hit
quite often, i was pretty good, spent afternoons making
clay spray into dust, and then one afternoon, clouds brewing,
a chickadee that had landed on one of the clay targets
sprayed into dust — aim raised just so,
a sob, stop, uncock

the ungrammaticality of the cameron street bridge

how long, go home, know
where things aren't to cost, tack
knowledge the least other, lose prior
ties the forest, water

gone city, curbs,
over jurisdiction, all
hush hush, not deal, finance-
tapped line, cut code,
you know, now

ledges spin & collision
cracks pavement, reclaims

the land stolen sounds off-
rhythm, haunting language

you hear it now, the street,
(1st ave. for one) that isn't one

after creeley's "for w.c.w."

the fragment
        more *there* than
  say   you

        *

then, too, the bastards
           spend themselves
           going *somewhere*

a record of the poet's
      insistence on context, repeating
     all that would

       *

writing
     the moment to crisis

the inverted tree (absurdity
  or a poetics of rage
 *trans*planting around the idea

what is given
to write

       *

what one wants is
what one wants
     some something or other

                the line   yours
carries
                    an adamant distance
                                            here

                        *

and then   without rage propping
            you

you stagger / with nothing in your arms

what bees see

designs in the infrastructure meant to disorient

chandeliers coming down

cadmium dust

surfaces of glass just before impact

the fear of embarrassment

scars on leaves

ultraviolet lines around your eyes

the pheromones of the truly sad

all manner of decay

that corduroy jacket that you were teased about in junior high

radio waves caught in loops

the breath of swallows and the pollen drifts from asia

semen stains on your pants

lines in the air made by the passage of time

disco balls and retro fashion of any kind

the last vestiges of hope before you release yourself to fate

all the blues and yellows that slip through our fingers

plastic toxins and all the ways they degrade

sparks of intuition

small stones that have been worn down by hands because they are child-
hood keepsakes that you will never forget

thought bubbles that never are recovered

chances to make things right, to establish order, to move forward into a
new era

fillings

laughter when it really means something

splits and fissures and faults — the frailty of matter — all the ways stone,
wood, air, ideas disintegrate

the very same thing I saw that spring morning by the side of the house by
the ferns and the musk of humus thawing

both peter pan and martyrdom complexes

not the colour green, so garish and compliant

the GMO flowers that taste like tuna

the furl and tilt of an antennae message sent this way and that

lists of things to do that will hold their form

line breaks and their function to send you another way where something
else might be found

the beauty of efficiency, simplicity, and elegance in the face of strange
breezes

the texture of the finest paper like fingerprints and the erogenous dance steps before they happen; the anticipation of elation

ant tracks, bird shadows, spider eyes

those substances that coagulate the spirit, make it hold together

map ink before it dries

dyes are a solution and are smaller than actual
colour on the molecular level. perception is held in suspension
and is considered a heterogeneous mixture.
poets and ideas are derived from
identical organic compounds. this similarity results
in ink classified as status.

functional polar groups are used
to working with dye molecules. this ingredient gives
power the disintegrating quality that is necessary to
dissolve the vehicle of class. that is what makes
that type of thought smaller.

with these functional polar groups, violence
is insoluble, the vehicles do not change from particle form.

to prevent the pigments from clustering, cooperating,
law makers must add a dispersing agent to the mixture.
the dispersing agent acts
as a detergent called order.

sea otter catches colonization under a rock, stanley park

still salty Salish air in fall
and the small flounder crunches
between her teeth

the otter numbers are up
not like stocks but spirits

she sits on a rock munching
the discourse called trade

that Spanish / Russian / British squeeze
in the straits when skins
came off with a sick sucking noise

globalization dribbles off her pelt,
her nonchalance, her pregnant belly,

this counter-colonial moment in
English Bay, the tide just turning

her satisfaction in being

to the university of northern bc hospital

addicted to
placeboes and the sound
tented over his laboured
breathing ...

a tube is inserted through his nose
to his stomach so he can
concentrate on language
unimpeded by saliva, taste, tongues ...

cancer is planted at the base of
his cerebral cortex — this
to accelerate his rhythm
and repeat his motifs — but
it makes poetry tired ...

medications come in many forms, the academic
sedative, the Beat stimulants, the hallucinogenics in
tiny thought balloons — nothing
really ever healed anything. The hospital
bed rode the purple waves ...

germs invade
the vents and siphons
into his system — he is
corrupted, nervous and
            circulating
                meaning slips
into fever,
                        delusional, he convulses, generates
a new form:

                a sleek,
                elegant twist of flesh
                the nurses don't see as
                the poem floats out the white window

civic planning 101

reconsidered the female muse
is unamused; she
is a writer, unused,
interdependent, and she shrugs
this off.

poetry is a truck she learns to drive
differently, somewhere else,
and then leaves it to the overgrowth.

'meaning' she said, meaning
it, and not the way you think, but
closer, and less esoteric, though
that's not the word she would use.

she realizes, if she only inspires,
she expires.

this muse is a juncture between.

she considers this point (a wave,
a particle) and muses on
luscious instability, works
at a university but does not
love it — closure
an alternative physiology
sensing herself for the first time.

poetry at unbc

the tuition was too obscure so he didn't. but
then later he was invited to read and he did,
carefully, wearing nothing but a body. the class
filmed everything for a documentary on
ethics, let him back into the wild as
unaltered as possible. during the reading,
hobo poem ducked through glass cases and found
himself matching his tone to the sounds of
heating ducts and plumbing — the building
applauded and his grades never made it
through the mail.

the tuition is in fake money anyway and the bookstore
imaginary. nutrients flow one way. water
is scarce.

he listens feverishly to the building's
blueprints that hover behind desks, disdainful
and dour.

the hill is unstable, but no one
seems to be concerned. information
flows still.

another poem's degree is major and she has no
recourse. plastic knowledge is her profession;
she plies it with grease and indecision. her pension
seeps into the ground.

a portable podium, he said
that's what we need, disembodied
on the stairs leading to
an unnecessary office.

the speech he made was a trifle, disorganizing
and sharp, a disruption of the office mail,
a swell in the corridor din.
all the while thinking of the number of inappropriate
things poetry could do right now.

sound vs. print

the veracity of meaning surprises him.
once, a crow imitation worked. what
was said was uncertain.

are you visualizing this moment?

time passes similarly; here he is
a wave from dockside sloshing
against speakers and paper
cuts the imagined spillage.
like feathers. yes,
it is a trick — what isn't?

the scientists test in dimensions of coffin, the variables
terrible and swift; the scientists
watch their lenses swim.

this is what first catches
crow's eye.

but singing is not in itself
freedom — the melody turns
on you, freedom singing itself
all the way to the bank.

the crow knows, berates
the poem, laughs and the
impossible 'f' sound changes crow's mind.

of the land

hung on the wrong word, a roadless
plan, a jettisoned part of something
else. the excess securities did not float. his arrival
in the place was reflexive, interdependent, economical
in a pre-historic way.

he began by relearning
pronouns and listening
to the dissertations of a glance, an anecdote.

the text, which was not one, did not lift free
like a pull-tab. he un-asserted himself, became
a slave, landless, literate.

off the land

slowly the place envelops
the needs and connections harden
in the soil of nouns. everything faces
the sun, rivulets down the trunk or
bank into what is necessary.

sitting still like this is
boring, it takes a lack of
imagination, and can draw fire.

know now the seasons
of ripe, the trails of hoof, the flash
of knowing animal in its many hides.

the valley runs
north-south and the wind
is the next stanzagraph.

rehab at awac

not many readers
left like antibodies and the town
has the shakes
and this empty space where
it was before returns

leaving town
leaving the collective
the addictive system
where positions remain
without people

rivers continue to run
underneath the street and
if left to, would sluice out
again taking away the parking
meters and sandwich shops

she has doubts on how
the drugs have affected memory
function and sensory
calmness can be settling
and unnerving

unnamed places

a twenty-first century polyp that
replicates at the treeline,

in a foreign country the travel
books of colonization are left
in tour buses and the next turn
is taken by smell, intuition

don't go back to the hotel

like the body, poetry leads or follows

my nomadic ancestry
follows the unencoded gaze of how
not why and when occurrences are now

that urge to walk into the woods

sometimes mammal, sometimes vegetable
sometimes malignant, poetry's growth can be
circumstantial, like itinerant ecologies of
the mind adjusting to the standard damage

a strategic
essentialism

the lack of history invades
more often than not, a disavowal of
the old ways, though sometimes
we long for the good story, the one
tucked away in plush condominium
lease agreements, the one
that designs the latest photo op,
the one destined for surefire fame

5th & george st.

and the history of the sign
that got us here, locked
chain-link barriers to the oversky

standing at the top
of some famous building, maybe
the Wood Innovation Centre, and looking through
one of those quarter binoculars
on the clunky swivel

you can imagine: the competition
for attention was multiple

the material word like this one
stands or scans and the moment,
like this one, takes a side

grain or rallies or trees or technique
and any hope of integration is lost

"what are you looking at?"

the answer is a matter of
selection, a field of vision
turned down to the small logo
pasted to the binoculars or
up sweeping up all the details
into a vision of the city and why

later, the poem answers,
"the commodification of social life"
but it's a little late
don't you think

the ten-storey plunge to the ground
is punctuated by a history of forms

nomad poem and the lime express

one cardboard box and which books
and maybe a writing job
when she gets there,
looking for something
inside elsewhere and buses
and trains rove through her
prose trying to evade a textual
body but all the kids are doing it

her body vibrates in anger
at the band, the lyrics a cut
into skin and her persona
throws ideas at ideas to
keep the demons away, to
make them stop — and they do

and one hits the drummer in the head a rim
shot and he rethinks the lyrics,
the position where he sits, power

her letter is signed by someone else
and her characters have hope
they will recover from culture someday

she is not sure how deep this trip
will take her and still can't fathom
diving and being,
really being, down there
and with who

moving day is a narrative
motif and closure is a myth

she leaves on Thursday but is
already gone and the transferable return fare
is a place in a novel
called home

the liberal

the social is a line
out front or in the book that changed
the way words looked but now
he finds his home in an ethical
moment — here and there — love and generosity tented
against the wind and mobile like
strange associations

camped outside the headquarters of
who and how long the murmurs
of mythical men who believe truly believe
and hurl epitaphs from large passing vehicles and Poem
wonders about that too while
ducking and continuing to prepare a
small meal

you see he doesn't want his way to hold
sway and won't try to convince you of what

anything means anything

this, he supposes
is the frightening part

this is a start

google sculpting on the prince george public library computers

how difficult it is for the poet to communicate reality with words

nations become what they produce

an industrial worker, relationship to socialist ideas, Al Purdy and Milton Acorn, the Allan Gardens free speech movement, Canadian cultural nationalism, and the politics of poets and poetry in times of social crisis

public agencies address the competing requirements for control and creativity

a drastic reduction in the adequacy of income support payments is key to the neoliberal agenda

releasing a part of one's self

as civilization advances, love for poetry declines; poetry in the modern context is trash

this site includes ads

further thoughts on the cultural labor of poetry and art

publishing your way at the price you want to pay

it seems to me that a lot of what happened in the September crash came from a system that rewarded people not for work, but for playing a kind of game

you may not be aware of all the places where poetry influences modern social values

the U.S. Embassy's Public Affairs Section organized a series of lectures and poetry reading sessions over a three-day program

the digital revolution makes the back-end invisible and therefore hard to quantify

as a rule of thumb, critics do not socialize with those they critique

the hills, the lochs, the black faced sheep, the Highland cows, the wild berries, etc. — in some parts, the farmed trees were so dense, your eyes had to adjust

the eleventh increment of the endless, the repeating decimals can (reasonably) claim to cover or embrace an everything

doddering infantilism

it all comes down to the marketplace in which we are all consumed

the movement of thoughts in the bowl

not like some baroque landscape or Group
of Seven epiphany, thoughts parasitic and un-
profound. poetry pulls them together like a
catalogue entry, an eBay ad for directions to
some imaginary city with wide avenues and no
traffic. at the post office on 5th, there is posted a 'most
wanted' poster for a perfect word, its history and
sound pattern. the path of flight is imaginary and
inward is the only direction. buttons and thimbles,
a letter unsent, three inkless pens, a compellation CD
sent late for his birthday; in ten years temperatures
will begin to sky-rocket. the lens changes the thing
is no longer. etymology and physiology are the same. or looping.
reconsidering the word "baroque" above and ah, and in that other city,
the air is clear and deep. cogito joins you for a walk.

the postmodern commute

part here, part there, past
his prime but plugged in,
hobo poem tries hard to do the right thing

the paradigms of mid-day
traffic just look bad
but remain in motion; poem sighs, edges out
on his refurbished bicycle using
proper hand signals and a dash
of theatre

poem is off to the printers and he
is an informed shopper,
rubs the linen texture between his fingers,
and looks for post-consumer
recycled paper whenever he can

the age thinks it's in transition but
poetry knows there is no such thing

if the moment exists,
an object is hurled out of a crew-cab
and the object "certainty" is not in flux

it hits him in the forehead, beneath his
properly adjusted helmet, and poem
falls beneath the wheel of what

when his eyes open poem looks up at
a kind pizza guy
cradling his head in his lap;
there is something familiar there but
publishers are a restless lot and
poem must hurry out of consciousness

he winks to the bystanders and takes
one final breath, there

prince george chamber of commerce

a review board convenes, votes
to lift the restrictions

lines on a map appear

for the prime investor, it is a coup, capital
flows into the machines

reading extracts the resources,
truck loads, driving unsafely on questionable roads,
filled with significance, leave
for the container ports, and markets
overseas send a cheque

but jobs are created, review
publications, chapters propped
up thriving on poetry's product,
that shining bin, that exasperating cargo

economic forecasters watch him,
his subsidiary paper product tax shelter,
and then, the vein is near
exhausted, the reserves spent,
the harvest dwindles and
the poem is left vacant

the road is abandoned,
saplings grow through the windows,
a wealth of rodents move in

'wait, wait
I can do other things —
look, this waste can become
something else useful or
I can be a call centre or, or
I can — I can sing!

but he is alone, a ghost
town echo

only the knowledge
that his wares, bobbles and
cheap lining material have traveled
the globe, filling drawers
and lost and found boxes

the poem rests, coos at the rafter
pigeons — it's okay, everything is okay

scripting the paths out

already considering the release, ready
all revved and contrite, poetry
finds himself stumbling toward

demise; death's fictive collage, a fatwa
pasted to our face, factions
coloured differently, flags, traffic signals
wrapped around the gaunt colonized quarter —
the course of writing follows
and feelings aren't order

a re-iteration, already considered
and accepted, yes, this is true,
this catafalque of meaning, besieged
and mounted on silt, sluiced away

stumbling to ward off stasis, semantic
availability — with a liquid gait the poem
strolls through the townhouses and
shopping plazas — stumbling in
limbic amniosis ...

already and always hunkered at the stop
light, gauges flaring and fuming ...

ideas leave the curb, a purge
off the left margin, clambering
across the busy current of syntax ...

an institution blares its horn

a systemic gridlock and the addition
of a new off-ramp into the Parkwood
Place parking lot, oh, what is poetry to ...

stumble forward. beliefs
split into asphalt. the light turns
opaque and doomed

the poem disappears, emphatic,
triumphant. evading the helicopter spotlights

poesis and 4th ave. office architecture

the poem contemplates the office walls
while he waits, avoids the report
in his lap, his own
diagnosis on cheap paper
and smudged ink

a self-same magnet, the force
split between sameness and
that one shout from the barrens

once a spectacle, once
a specimen, he becomes

otherwise he'd just be

— so this scientist walks into
the bar, leans into
the discourse, justifies
the means, jars
and translations skitter across
the limbic scythe

& lands: hope, anxiety, fear,
nostalgia, guilt, hate
give chase, a posse

or sexuality, a dream
where he just is

this nomenclature, nodal,
a clandestine swoop through
the once was —

& lands, where I am speaking from
is a hinge into and from,
and two-sided, neither
stable; digression is another

shifting his weight
on the chair, he refocuses on
his book — he is rereading
this passage, trying to flick
away a housefly, bumping
against the sound of the word

other, which is somewhere else,
far away in an unlivable valley,
and the place fills with indecision —
though not the simple kind — and
where is not exactly sure but

still, some thing occurs; the poem,
at least, is sure of it — recovers
his jacket, steps away from the recent
tools, looks for the nearest exit.

emergency via edmonton street

prosthetics of thought wrought
in post-op — the reconstruction zone:

*one poem is in dense
clothing, the weight warm
as the lab coats lead her out
to the white white van.*

the measure thrown
off and despite that phantom
limb they keep saying how
great everything is
and how about those canucks ...

the turns taken from the writing
when form colludes to lift
agency from the page, when
the bureaucracy of the text takes over

*another poem, the automaton cranes his neck to see
what was missed, where they are taking her,
where the cut will be deepest,
why 'will' is just the future tense ...*

a minor death, authenticity,
when all the charts say it
must be so

the hospital air is sucked
dry of germs and
expectation of anything else

*another poem is under
a thick anesthetic and this
produces a new age of art.*

where are the advocates? where
are the warriors? a hum-like
dirge is all that we hear

this poem does not make it —
asphyxiates in transit —
and is pronounced 2:13 a.m.

poetry and I meet for coffee

he arrives on an alternate
clock-time, walking from his house
where he lives with politics and
questions. often this is so.

we are here
at a moment of danger.

the returning steelhead recognized him;
listening for what
is happening. and twenty years ago
I was that fish looking up
a vowel tickling gravel. .

the coffee shop, a second order
description, enjambs the time
open. hand shaped word.

we sit between you — a figure
of outward. those paths
were there before, still are
but less and more powerful.

poetry saved us from
the street, so we can sit, talking
into the writing otherwise.

he and I, a relationship
of culture, a contact zone where
poetics curl from matter, coffee
a problem, the land's content
and form calling, we, a school
of language landing here.

prince george city council

moving with little assurance,
poetry rises, visibly
shaken and begins his address to council

drawn out, an inevitable push, the politics
is not unlike the clearing of land

(away in the distance
there is another voice
a wavering echo in another
language)

conviction is second growth
and cities are not built to last —
air, water, and forest is an idea-
shaped company

nouns would mean nothing, like
wood that stands for no idea but
stay stay stay, falling for none
of our elaborate causes or the way
poems end well

a hope grows
that the land would have us back

until then, the scene is set
   — the hunting rambler, a beautiful trophy,
a small consolation
in a sad artful epidemic

meanwhile, the tensions in the room are
many and the security guards
scribble reviews to print
in the college newspaper

he is not being understood;
city council is an idea-
shaped room with no windows

poem clears his throat again
tries another sound

but the motion is defeated

logging town memoirs

the way out
is not south
even if you ride a log
down you will not arrive

this is the state
of colonization — we reside, spool
another ream of paper in a mill
where nothing arrives and nothing
leaves — this still
economy, one black
and blue with pain-
painted trucks and their
airborne residues

and he stands askance as the paper dries
and writes blurred letters as fast as he can

it is, of course, unsellable but
valuable as hell — I for one
can't wait to see it ...

as the decades roll by
trees get slow slower
and stop falling and the air clears;
we redevelop the downtown
around a lack
of ownership and a sense
of a collective uncertain sigh

we are home

this is called living
in a logging town
and shutting it down

unstable, after the end

camped outside the silent compound, living
on wild onion and soap
berries, the new
coursing through — information
in now not viable — satellites wobble
because the ragged militia all
died out and we believe less, believe in
loss — the park is less dense with thistle and loose-
strife, the toxins are not yet
over — contact is lost — we are
grown uncontrolled, un-
cultured, crouch, haunches quivering,
chew on a poorly preserved
protein bar, check bellies
for signs of the blight — nothing
flies over — flies hover
everywhere — cattle corpses
pile up in the bog — factories
become aesthetic

paper is difficult here, post-
consumer but degrading quickly the words
hard to come by — we carried
the dead laptop for a year before
it skidded down the impassable
riverbank — different circuits work
now, scents and small noises — even
consonants become obsolete

we may
or may not survive — this is
a good thing for poetry,
a good sign

acknowledgements

Hugs to my kids — Robin, Erin, Quin, and Anya — who continue to inspire and surprise. Thank you to Irene Nelson, Ken Belford, and Si Transken for their love and creativity.

Some of these poems have appeared, in various forms, in:

Dreamland Theatre (chapbook). Prince George: wink books, 2010.

Dusie 10: the Canadian issue. Ed. rob mclennan. June 20, 2010 volume 3, number 2. http://www.dusie.org/pdfs/dusie10.pdf.

The Enpipe Line: 70,000+ Kilometers of Poetry Written in Resistance to the Enbridge Northern Gateway Pipelines Proposal. Ed. Christine Leclerc, Jen Currin et al. Smithers: Creekstone Press, 2012.

ROB BUDDE teaches creative writing at the University of Northern British Columbia in Prince George. He has published seven books (poetry, novels, interviews and short fiction) and appeared in numerous literary magazines including *Canadian Literature, The Capilano Review, West Coast Line, Dusie, ditch, filling Station, Prairie Fire, Matrix,* and *dandelion.* He is also a regular columnist for *Northword Magazine.* His most recent books are *declining america* from BookThug and *Finding Ft. George* from Caitlin Press.

Dreamland Theatre is typeset in Arno Pro. Designed by Robert Slimbach, Arno was crafted in the tradition of early Venetian and Aldine book types. Named after the river that runs through Florence, the center of the Italian Renaissance, Arno draws on the warmth and readability of early humanist types of the 15th and 16th centuries.